Cheetahs
For Kids

Amazing Animal Books
For Young Readers

By
Rachel Smith

Mendon Cottage Books
JD-Biz Corp Publishing

Download Free Books!
http://MendonCottageBooks.com

Read More Amazing Animal Books

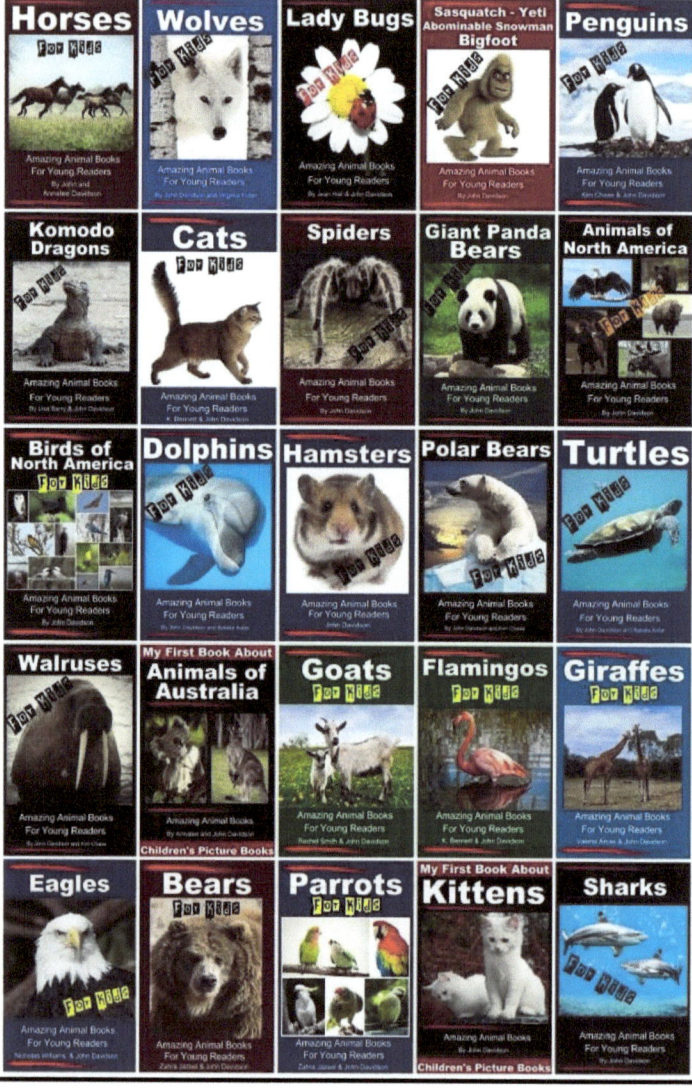

Purchase at Amazon.com

Table of Contents

Introduction

Cheetahs are probably one of the lesser known big cats. The tiger and the lion are the best known, no doubt about that; however, cheetahs definitely have their own space in the world's cultures.

As the fastest land animal alive, the cheetah has enchanted many people throughout history. From the people who have had them around as long as they can remember, to the explorers who saw them for the first time, the cheetah captured the imagination of people everywhere.

The cheetah lives in many parts of Africa, as well as Iran. It used to be that the cheetah also lived in a good portion of Asia, including India, but it was pushed out. Still, the cheetah is well remembered there, and there is an effort to reintroduce the cheetah, which was pushed out in the 1940's.

What is a cheetah?

A cheetah is a big cat, to be short. However, there is a lot more that goes into the cheetah identity than just being a big cat. The big cats consist of the leopard, jaguar, snow leopard, tiger, lion, and of course, the cheetah. The cheetah is probably the smallest, and certainly the least physically strong.

A cheetah mother and her cub.

Cheetahs are not built to be strong, at least not when you compare them to their fellow big cats. Jaguars are basically lumps of muscle; lions and tigers are probably some of the strongest carnivores alive. The cheetah, on the other hand, is built for speed, and thus, it is much skinnier and more delicate-looking.

The cheetah is the only living member of the genus Acinonyx. There were a number of members of this family in the past, including the giant cheetah. The giant cheetah was twice the size of the modern cheetah, at about the same height as a lion. Then, there was also another cheetah that was 'discovered' in the 21st century, but this was determined to be a fake.

The only other two members of this genus are also extinct, and discovered in the 20th century.

Interestingly, there were also American cheetahs many, many years ago. These animals lived in a very similar habitat to the cheetah, and so developed similarly. However, they were not related. This is a case of what's called convergent evolution, which means that two animals evolved the same way in completely different places, but aren't related.

Evolution is when an animal (including humans) change over time. This process is hotly debated among scientists, with many holding that entirely different species can come from one kind, and others holding that only small changes can come about. Still others insist there is no evolution. That's an argument for a different book, however.

Cheetahs are very slight animals, meaning that they are skinny. Their chests are deep, to allow for a lot of air to be taken in, but their waists are skinny.

A cheetah is covered in spots, generally speaking. Their fur is kind of rough, a golden color with black spots. Their tail is also spotted, but ends in four to six black rings, and a white tuft. Their underside is white.

This spotting is for camouflage; it helps the cheetah blend in, because it certainly isn't the biggest predator in its habitat. The cheetah is not the top of the food chain.

It also has what look like black tear tracks down its face, as well as somewhat around its eyes. This is so that it can see without the sun getting in its eyes. The black absorbs the light, and keeps it from reflecting into the cheetah's eyes.

Cheetahs don't have much variety in genetics. What are genetics? Genetics are what make up any living thing; genes determine everything from the moment a being is conceived, from their hair or fur color to having all four limbs or so on. Genes are like a blueprint for your cells to build from.

Humans, for example, have a lot of variety in genes. From all the hair colors, skin colors, eye colors, and other small things, to things like the ability to survive the black plague or not get leprosy, humans vary all over the world.

On the other hand, cheetahs vary very little. Where humans must have a match with someone to have a successful skin graft, such as their sibling or parent, a cheetah can typically use a graft from any other cheetah. They are all so close genetically that it makes little difference.

This is a problem for the cheetah, because the problem with little differences is that if a big disease struck them, it might turn out that none of them had resistance, and they would all die out. This hasn't happened with humans due to our variation; the black death, a plague back during medieval times, wiped out two thirds of Europe's population, but because some people had the quirk of not succumbing to it, the people survived.

Cheetahs are built for speed, but not long distance speed.. Their best ability, rather than their speed, is their agility. You know how when you start running really fast, it can be hard to stop or change direction? A cheetah can slow itself a lot in one stride, as well as change direction fairly easily.

Males are typically bigger than females, and have some differences in their teeth and their skull. Other than that, it can be very hard to tell male and female cheetahs apart.

The reason a cheetah can run so fast is not just its body, however. Other things contribute.

When you're using a lot of energy like when running very fast, you use up oxygen. So, a cheetah has to take in more oxygen and use it better than the average creature. One way they do this is through large nostrils.

Another way is through their heart and lungs; for their size, they are very big, and are very good at efficiently pumping oxygen throughout the cheetah's body. They are able to keep the cheetah from, for example, fainting when they go extremely fast.

It also uses its tail as a sort of rudder; a rudder is a part on a ship that steers it. Basically, the cheetah uses its tail to offset its momentum. Lastly, it has great traction; its claws are semi-retractable, meaning it can partly pull them in. These claws make for a great way of gripping the ground when necessary.

The cheetah can purr, but not roar. Interestingly, pretty much ever other big cat can roar, but not purr. Still, the cheetah is considered by most to be a big cat despite this difference.

A cheetah is a very shy animal, and also has a very hard time adapting. In zoos, this is often a problem.

How do cheetahs act?

One important thing to know is that there is a big difference between male and female behavior. Cheetahs may not look so different between sexes, but they are incredibly different in terms of socializing and other behaviors.

A cheetah running.

Males tend to live in groups. These groups are usually made up of brothers, but if there was only one male in the litter, then the lone male might find other lone males and group up with them. Males are far more social than females.

The males tend to live in a territory, which they mark with urine or feces, and then guard it to the death against other males. They will unreservedly kill any male cheetah that tries to enter it or hunt in it.

The main point with these territories is that they're on the edges of female home ranges. Males want the opportunity to mate, since that is their biological drive, like pretty much any creature that doesn't reproduce asexually. The main purpose of existing, for most animals, is to keep their species alive. Of course, it's not a conscious thought in animals; it's a part of their nature. Animals' brains don't work quite the same as humans, but we still don't know for sure just how different they are.

Females, on the other hand, will never be in a group. The only exception to this rule is, of course, looking after their cubs. Female cheetahs don't establish territories; instead, they have home ranges.

A home range is a wide swath of habitat, much bigger than a male cheetah's territory. However, a female cheetah's home range can and usually does overlap with other female cheetahs' home ranges. These other female cheetahs are typically their mothers, daughters, or sisters.

Then, with cheetahs, there's a lot of vocalization, or making sounds. All these sounds and such are not exactly clear; not a lot of recordings and such have been made, and they haven't been studied incredibly closely.

However, there are several sounds most zoologists agree on.

One is chirping. Chirping is a sort of short, high-pitched bark, used to find other cheetahs; most of the time, this is a mother looking for her cubs. Then, there's also the chirping noise that cubs make, which is a lot more like birds chirping.

Churring, also known as stuttering, is a little harder to describe. It's not a growl, and it's not a chirp, but it tends to be a friendly sound. However, the two sexes make this noise for different reasons, ranging from an invitation to be social to uncertainty.

Obviously, there's growling, which usually has a lot of hissing or spitting. This turns into yowling if there's enough danger, which is louder and more aggressive; it also involves more spitting, which is something cheetahs are fairly well known for.

Then there's purring. Purring is a happy sound, though it's typically only made by cubs with their mother. Cubs that purr are generally completely content and happy.

Cheetahs are carnivores. This means they absolutely must eat meat. Meat is an essential part of their diet, and they can't survive without it. Unlike omnivores, which can eat just about anything, or herbivores, which survive on plants, the carnivore must consume the flesh of other creatures.

The main source of food for cheetahs is the antelope. There's a wide variety of antelopes, as that's an umbrella term for a huge group of herbivores. They are also known to go after: bat-eared foxes, ostriches, warthogs, zebras, and more, though these are much more rare. They much prefer medium-sized animals that are very bad at fighting back.

Cheetahs hunt by sight, not by scent. This means they usually hunt only under good sight conditions; they also prefer to hunt when it's less hot out. Cheetahs tend to sneak up on their prey, within a short distance, and then they start the chase.

The chase begins and is over with within a minute. If a cheetah can't make a kill within a minute, it simply gives up. It doesn't want to waste energy on a hard kill.

A cheetah's main strategy is to chase its prey, and then trip it. Once the prey is brought down, it clamps its teeth on its neck, and then it suffocates the animal. Sometimes it cuts an important artery (blood vessel) too, but that's a coincidence more than anything.

The cheetah must eat its prey quickly, because bigger or stronger predators may try to take it; also, klepoparasites, which are animals that try to steal kills from other animals, may work together to try to take the cheetah's kill.

About half the time, a cheetah manages to kill its prey.

Cheetahs will not fight to keep their prey. If even one hyena comes after it, they will give it up. Why? Because their speed is at the expense of strength, which leaves them vulnerable to other predators. Also, if the cheetah is injured at all, in any way that affects its speed, it might not be able to hunt anymore, and it will starve. It simply can't risk getting hurt if it can help it.

A male and female cheetah don't mate for life. In fact, a female cheetah's litter may have more than one father, on rare occasions. A mother will keep her litter with her for over a year, at which point the cubs depart and are independent.

A mother cheetah will typically have six cubs. The high number is because a large amount of the cubs end up dying before even reaching independence; cheetah cubs are considered a good meal by many predators, from lions to African wild dogs.

To protect from these predators, a cheetah cub is born with a mantle. This mantle is a bunch of bluish fur that kind of stands up like a mohawk; some have suggested that this is to make them look more like honey badgers, an aggressive animal no other animal wants to mess with. Others say this is a camouflage thing instead, and the mantle helps the cubs blend in to their environment.

What kinds of cheetahs are there?

There are a few subspecies of cheetahs. They are specific to their habitats, or the general area they live in.

A cheetah from Kenya.

The key thing to understand about subspecies is that a subspecies is definitely not a separate animal. It's still very much a cheetah, and would not be classified as anything else. A subspecies is just a way to make clear the differences between different populations of the animal.

Many kinds of animals, any with a wide range, tend to have a number of subspecies.

For cheetahs, this number is five.

Firstly, there's the South African cheetah. It lives in South Africa, the country, but also in surrounding southern African countries. This cheetah has severely dropped in its range and numbers, and is in endangered to an extent.

Then there's the Tanzanian cheetah. This one is the second most populous, with the South African being the most. The Tanzanian cheetah lives in other parts of Africa, and as with all cheetahs, it lives in grasslands. This one tends to have an especially high rate of cub deaths in several of its protected areas.

The Sudan cheetah is nearly identical to the South African cheetah, but there appear to be small genetic differences. This type of cheetah is the second-largest, and there are only about two thousand in the wild.

The Northwest African cheetah is one of the most endangered kinds of cheetah, with only about two hundred and fifty left. It's the smallest and palest kind of cheetah, and is critically endangered.

However, even worse off is the Asiatic cheetah. This animal once lived throughout places like Saudi Arabia, India, and so on; now, it only lives in a few of Iran's national parks, numbering at probably fifty or seventy total. It's sometimes called the Iranian or Indian cheetah, but the Asiatic cheetah as a name reflects its previous wider range. It's the only cheetah that lives outside of Africa. It also is the only cheetah to have a woolly, thick winter coat.

The history of cheetahs and humans

Cheetahs and humans have quite the history—modern and past.

A cheetah within an enclosure in Namibia, Africa.

For one thing, the taming of cheetahs goes way back. Cheetahs are fairly easy to tame compared to their fellow big cats, given that they are far more likely to flee than they are to fight. The exception to this being in protection of cubs, of course. But, cheetahs are remarkably shy and unlikely to attack a human.

Ancient Egyptians tamed cheetahs quite frequently, training them to aid in hunts—but the key thing to know here is that the cheetah, unlike the dog and the house cat, was not domesticated. That is, it wasn't bred selectively until it would no longer be resistant to humans; the dog we have now is the product of untold generations of breeding and molding. The cheetah went through no such thing.

The Ancient Egyptians would simply bring them alongside their hunting chariots, and keep them blindfolded while the hunting dogs flushed out the prey. Then, when the moment was ripe, the cheetahs would be released, and they would take down the prey.

A lot of cheetahs have been tamed in the past and present. For one thing, such famous historical figures as Genghis Khan—the Mongol conqueror whose military prowess led to the largest empire ever—and Charlemagne, a king of early France, both boasted of having pet cheetahs that roamed their palaces.

The Persians and the Indians (of India, not Native America) also kept cheetahs, though they mostly stuck to the same formula as the Ancient Egyptians in using them as hunting animals. Indian princes were very fond of having cheetahs, as this was a sign of wealth and prowess, and so some were known to boast of having over a thousand cheetahs at their disposal.

Even more recently, the cheetah was as sign of elegance and royalty. Haile Selassie, who was the Emperor of Ethiopia, an African nation that would be embroiled in colonialism and war during his lifetime, was often photographed with a cheetah on a leash in the 1930's, before everything went downhill.

Nowadays, cheetahs are still kept as pets—but for the most part, this is very illegal. It's easy enough to find cheetah cubs for sale if you know where to look, but these cheetah cubs rarely survive long, and in general being forced to be pets is very bad for them.

Cheetahs kept in zoos and other places also face challenges. For one thing, cheetahs don't breed very well. They are often far too nervous to breed in captivity, since they are taken outside of their normal home and such.

One solution has been to give each cheetah its own dog. These dogs are trained to take care of the cheetah and bond with them, and they keep them from getting too stressed, which is easy to do when you're a cheetah.

Cheetahs and conservation

Cheetahs are in a considerable amount of danger, especially considering some of the subspecies. However, measures can be taken to protect them.

A cheetah mother and her two young ones—nearly ready to leave.

One big issue with cheetahs is the worry among geneticists that cheetahs are just too in-bred. In-bred is when a group of any kind of breeding animal doesn't have enough variety; it would be like only having people who were already related, at least a little, to populate an area. You get problems, which is evident in the cheetah and the large amount of problems cubs are often born with.

However, the thought is also that the decline of cheetahs has only occurred recently, even though their diversity tanked thousands of years ago.

So, the cause is most likely human.

And a lot of causes there are. For one thing, habitat is being destroyed at an alarming rate. Like many animals in Africa and throughout the world, the cheetah is finding itself getting more and more enclosed. With less space, there have to be less cheetahs, because there isn't enough territory to support them.

Another cause is the conflicts between humans and cheetahs. Since there's less space for all animals, more aggressive predators have been pushing cheetahs out—and into human territory, such as farms. So, farmers tend to react badly to cheetahs, often hurting or killing them.

Lastly, as previously mentioned, there's the illegal trade of cheetahs— not just cubs, but also furs. It's despicable, given there are only about ten thousand left in the wild. The people who are desperate enough to hunt cheetahs should not be blamed, however, as these people are often poor; the people who should be blamed are the ones who make a demand for the cheetahs, because if no one was buying, no one would be selling.

Morphs and other differences among cheetahs

Morphs are when there's a different kind of coat or fur appearance than the normal kind. It's not a mutation or anything unusual, it's just a more rare version of a cheetah.

A king cheetah

The morph for a cheetah is the king cheetah morph. This type of cheetah is generally just a little bigger and more powerful, but the biggest difference is its coat: it has thick patterns of black, sort of making stripes and connecting spots. It was thought, for a very long time, that the king cheetah was a separate species, or even a made up creature, but it has since been found to be real, just rare.

A cheetah can also have other coat differences, from melanisism (black) to chinchillism(a sort of grayish color) to albinism (total lack of color, making them appear white). Of course, there are a lot more, but these would take a while to go over.

Conclusion

The cheetah has its problems, but is worth saving. It's a beautiful creature that deserves a chance.

From the cheetahs we know and love as cartoony characters, to the tame cheetahs who travel the world, cheetahs will probably long have an effect on the world.

We can only hope they stay around long enough not to become similar to the dodo bird.

Author Bio

Rachel Smith is a young author who enjoys animals. Once, she had a rabbit who was very nervous, and chewed through her leash and tried to escape. She's also had several pet mice, who were the funniest little animals to watch. She lives in Ohio with her family and writes in her spare time.

Publisher

JD-Biz Corp

P O Box 374

Mendon, Utah 84325

http://www.jd-biz.com/

Top Ten Dog Breeds For Kids

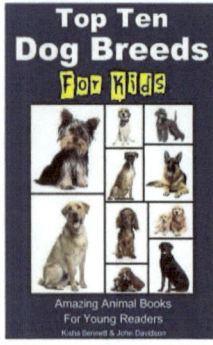

Amazing Animal Books For Young Readers
Kisha Bennett & John Davidson

German Shepherds

Dog Books for Kids
K. Bennett

Bulldogs

Dog Books for Kids
K. Bennett

Dachshund

Dog Books for Kids
K. Bennett

Poodles

Dog Books for Kids
K. Bennett

Labrador Retrievers

Dog Books for Kids
K. Bennett

Rottweilers

Dog Books for Kids
K. Bennett

Boxers

Dog Books for Kids
K. Bennett

Golden Retrievers

Dog Books for Kids
K. Bennett

Puppies
Dog Books For Kids

Amazing Animal Books
By John Davidson

Beagles

Dog Books for Kids
K. Bennett

Yorkshire Terriers

Dog Books for Kids
K. Bennett

Dogs
Top Ten Dog Breeds For Kids

Amazing Animal Books
For Young Readers
Zahra Jazeel & John Davidson

Cats For Kids

Amazing Animal Books
For Young Readers
K. Bennett & John Davidson

Foxes For Kids

Amazing Animal Books
For Young Readers
Zahra Jazeel & John Davidson

Wolves For Kids

Amazing Animal Books
For Young Readers
By John Davidson and Virginia Fidler

Our books are available at

1. Amazon.com

2. Barnes and Noble

3. Itunes

4. Kobo

5. Smashwords

6. Google Play Books

Download Free Books!
http://MendonCottageBooks.com

www.ingramcontent.com/pod-product-compliance
Lightning Source LLC
Chambersburg PA
CBHW050911290526
45792CB00002B/780